# 100 FACTS

# Human Body

# 100 FACTS

# Human Body

Steve Parker

Consultant: Dr. Kristina Routh MB ChB

Sandy Creek
NEW YORK

An Imprint of Sterling Publishing
387 Park Avenue South
New York, NY 10016

Publishing Director Belinda Gallagher
Creative Director Jo Cowan
Editorial Assistant Lauren White
Designer Kayleigh Allen
Indexer Jane Parker
Production Manager Elizabeth Collins
Reprographics Stephan Davis, Jennifer Hunt
Image Manager Liberty Newton
Assets Lorraine King

ISBN 978-1-4351-5091-1


## ACKNOWLEDGMENTS

The publishers would like to thank the following artists who have contributed to this book:
Syd Brak, Mike Foster/Maltings Partnership, Janos Marffy, Martin Sanders, Mike Saunders, Rudi Vizi

Cartoons by Mark Davis at Mackerel

All other artwork from the Miles Kelly Artwork Bank

The publisher would like to thank the following sources for the use of their photographs:
t = top, b = bottom, l = left, r = right, bg = background

Front cover: Sciepro/Science Photo Library/Corbis, Back cover: Andrea Danti/Shutterstock.com
**Dreamstime** 9(b) Alangh; 10(b) Velkol; 25 Tobkatrina; 31 Kati1313; 43 Barsik
**Fotolia** 19 chrisharvey; 21 Alexander Yakovlev; 39(r) Andres Rodriguez
**iStockphoto.com** 11(b) Rosemarie Gearhart **Shutterstock** Back cover: James Doss;
5(b) Linda Bucklin; 6–7 6(tl) jan kranendonk; 6(tl) Jurgen Ziewe; 11(t) Kozlovskaya Ksenia;
12 Lilya Espinosa; 13 Stanislav Fridkin; 14(blonde) Jeanne Hatch, (straight black) wong sze yuen;
(curly black) Felix Mizioznikov; 15(l) Steven Chiang, (r) Carmen Steiner; 18 konmesa;
22–23 PiLart; 22 Taranova; 23 Jaren Jai Wicklund; 24 JonMilnes; 27 Lawrence Wee;
28–29 Elena Schweitzer; 28(bl) Yuri Arcurs; 31 Kati1313; 34–35(bg) Sebastian Kaulitzki;
37(tr) beerkoff; 39(l) Paul Matthew Photography; 41 Elena Elisseeva; 45 Sebastien Burel;
46 picturepartners; 47 Monkey Business Images

All other photographs are from: PhotoDisc

Every effort has been made to acknowledge the source and copyright holder of each picture.
Miles Kelly Publishing apologizes for any unintentional errors or omissions.

Made with paper from a sustainable forest

Manufactured in China
Lot #:
2 4 6 8 10 9 7 5 3 1

# Contents

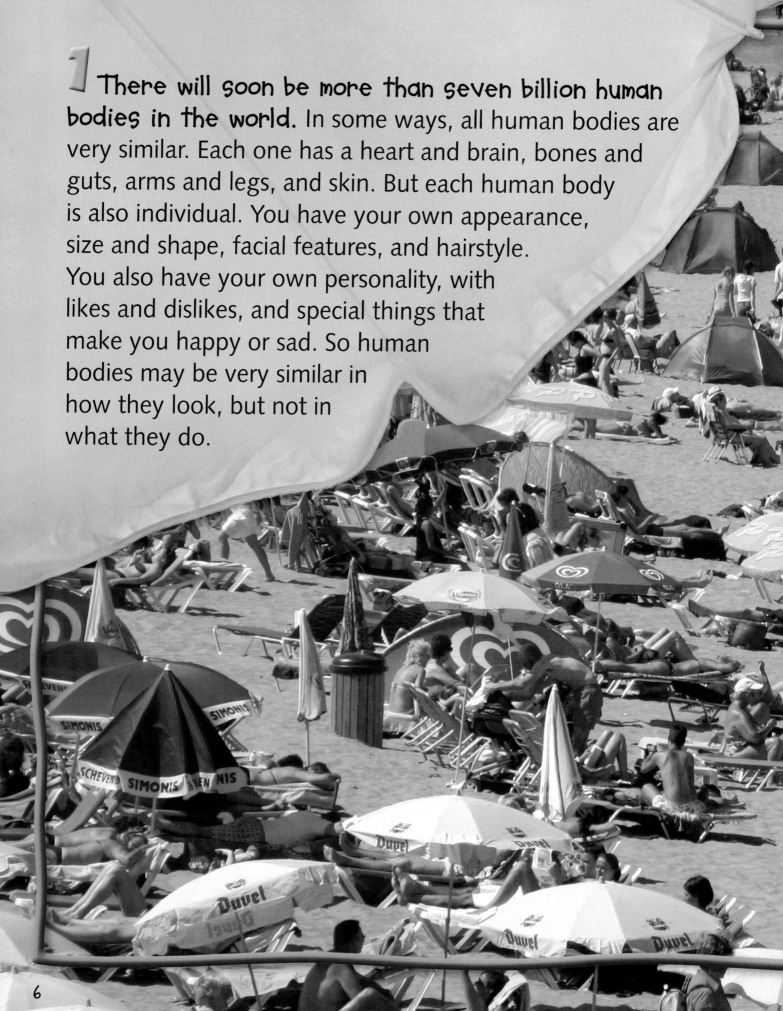

# Outside, inside

**1** **There will soon be more than seven billion human bodies in the world.** In some ways, all human bodies are very similar. Each one has a heart and brain, bones and guts, arms and legs, and skin. But each human body is also individual. You have your own appearance, size and shape, facial features, and hairstyle. You also have your own personality, with likes and dislikes, and special things that make you happy or sad. So human bodies may be very similar in how they look, but not in what they do.

▲ We tend to notice small differences between people, such as height, body shape, hair color, and clothes. This allows us to recognize our family and friends.

# Baby body

Successful sperm

Egg cell

**2** A full-grown human body is made of billions of microscopic parts, called cells. But in the beginning, the body is a miniscule single cell. Yet it contains all the instructions, known as genes, for the whole body to grow and develop.

Wall of uterus

Fluid around baby

Bones of skeleton start to form

Hair begins to grow on head

Placenta (afterbirth)

Two months

Face has taken shape

Three months

Umbilical cord

Baby begins to move and kick

Five months

Seven months

▲▶Thousands of sperm cells reach the egg (top), but only one is successful and joins with it, at fertilization. This starts the growth of the baby, shown here after two, three, five, seven, and nine months.

**3** The body begins when an egg cell inside the mother joins up with sperm from the father. The egg cell splits into two cells, then into four cells, then eight, and so on. The bundle of cells embeds itself in the mother's womb (uterus), which protects and nourishes it. Soon there are thousands of cells, then millions, forming a tiny embryo. After two months the embryo has grown into a tiny baby, as big as your thumb, with arms, legs, eyes, ears, and a mouth.

Umbilical cord

Wall of womb is stretched

Placenta

Baby is born head first

Nine months

Cervix (neck of womb)

**4** After nine months in the womb, the baby is ready to be born. Strong muscles in the walls of the womb tighten, or contract. They push the baby through the opening, or neck of the womb, called the cervix, and along the birth canal. The baby enters the outside world.

**5** A newborn baby may be frightened and usually starts to cry. Inside the womb it was warm, wet, dark, quiet, and cramped. Outside there are lights, noises, voices, fresh air, and room to stretch. The crying is also helpful to start the baby breathing, using its own lungs.

**6** Being born can take an hour or two—or a whole day or two. It is very tiring for both the baby and its mother. After birth, the baby starts to feel hungry and it feeds on its mother's milk. Finally, mother and baby settle down for a rest and some sleep.

## I DON'T BELIEVE IT!

The human body never grows as fast again as it does during the first weeks in the womb. If the body kept growing at that rate, every day for 50 years, it would be bigger than the biggest mountain in the world!

▲ Once the baby is settled it is time for its mother to admire her newborn and rest.

# The growing body

**7** A new baby just seems to eat, sleep, and cry. It feeds on milk when hungry and sleeps when tired. Also, it cries when it is too hot, too cold, or when its diaper needs changing.

## WHAT HAPPENS WHEN?

Most babies learn to do certain actions in the same order. The order is mixed up here. Can you put it right?

walk, crawl, roll over, sit up, smile, stand

Answers:
smile, roll over, sit up, crawl, stand, walk

▼ In the grasping reflex, the baby tightly holds anything that touches its hand or fingers. Its grip is surprisingly strong!

**8** A new baby is not totally helpless. It can do simple actions called reflexes, to help it survive. If something touches the baby's cheek, it turns its head to that side and tries to suck. If the baby hears a loud noise, it opens its eyes wide, throws out its arms, and cries for help. If something touches the baby's hand and fingers, it grasps tightly.

**9** A new baby looks, listens, touches, and quickly learns. Gradually it starts to recognize voices, faces, and places. After about six weeks, it begins to smile. The baby's brain is learning quickly and will soon know that if it laughs, people will laugh back and if it cries, someone will come to look after it.

▼ Most babies crawl before they walk, but some go straight from sitting or "bottom-shuffling" to walking.

**11** As a baby grows into a child, at around 18 months, it learns many new words each day, from "cat" and "dog" to "sun" and "moon." There are new games such as piling up bricks, new actions such as throwing and kicking, and new skills such as using a spoon at mealtimes.

**10** At about three months old, most babies can reach out to hold something, and roll over when lying down. By the age of six months, most babies can sit up and hold food in their fingers. At nine months, many babies are crawling well and perhaps standing up. By their first birthday, many babies are learning to walk and starting to talk.

**12** At five years old, when most children start school, they continue to learn quickly. This includes thinking or mental skills such as counting and reading, and precise movements such as writing and drawing. They learn out of the classroom too—how to play with friends and share.

▼ Playing is lots of fun, but it's learning too, as children develop control over the muscles in their fast-growing bodies.

# On the body's outside

**13** The surface of our skin is made of tiny cells that have filled up with a hard, tough substance called keratin, and then died. So when you look at a human body, most of what you see is "dead!" The cells get rubbed off as you move, have a wash, and get dry.

**14** Skin rubs off and grows all the time. Just under the surface, living cells make more new cells that gradually fill with keratin, die, and move up to the surface. It takes about four weeks from a new skin cell being made to when it reaches the surface and is rubbed off. This upper layer of skin is the epidermis.

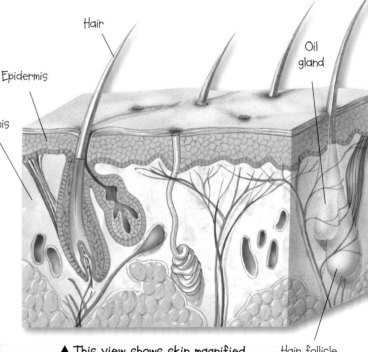

Hair

Oil gland

Epidermis

Dermis

Hair follicle

▲ This view shows skin magnified (enlarged) about 50 times.

▲ Lots of dead skin is removed without you realizing when you dry yourself after a shower.

**15** The skin's lower layer, the dermis, is thicker than the the epidermis. It is made of tiny, flexible, threadlike fibers of the substance collagen. The dermis also contains small blood vessels, tiny sweat glands, and microsensors that detect touch.

**16** One of the skin's important jobs is to protect the body. It stops the delicate inner parts from being rubbed, knocked, or scraped. Skin also prevents body fluids from leaking away and it keeps out dirt and germs.

**17** Skin helps to keep the body at the same temperature. If you become too hot, sweat oozes onto your skin and, as it dries, draws heat from the body. Also, the blood vessels in the lower layer of skin widen, to lose more heat through the skin. This is why a hot person looks sweaty and red in the face.

**18** Skin gives us our sense of touch. Millions of microscopic sensors in the lower layer of skin, the dermis, are joined by nerves to the brain. These sensors detect different kinds of touch, from a light stroke to heavy pressure, heat or cold, and movement. Pain sensors detect when skin is damaged. Ouch!

Safety helmet protects head and brain

Elbow-pads cushion fall

Gloves save fingers from scrapes and breaks

Knee-pads prevent hard bumps

▲ Skin is tough, but it sometimes needs help to protect the body. Otherwise it, and the body parts beneath, may get damaged.

## SENSITIVE SKIN

**You will need:**

a friend   sticky-tack
two used matchsticks   ruler

1. Press some sticky-tack on the end of the ruler. Press two matchsticks into the sticky-tack, standing upright, about half an inch apart.

2. Make your friend look away. Touch the back of their hand with both matchstick ends. Ask your friend: "Is that one matchstick or two?" Sensitive skin can detect both ends.

3. Try this at several places, such as on the finger, wrist, forearm, neck, and cheek.

# Hair and nails

**19** There are about 120,000 hairs on the head, called scalp hairs. There are also eyebrow hairs and eyelash hairs. Adults have hairs in the armpits and between the legs, and men have hairs on the face. And everyone, even a baby, has tiny hairs all over the body—5 to 10 million of them!

Blonde wavy hair is the result of carotene from an oval hair follicle

Black curly hair is the result of black melanin from a flat hair follicle

Straight red hair is the result of red melanin from a round hair follicle

◄ Hair contains pigments (colored substances)—mainly melanin (dark brown) and some carotene (yellowish). Different amounts of pigments, and the way their tiny particles are spread out, cause different hair colors.

**20** Each hair grows from a deep pit in the skin, called a follicle. The hair is only alive where it gets longer, at its base or root, in the bottom of the follicle. The rest of the hair, called the shaft, is like the surface of the skin—hard, tough, dead, and made of keratin. Hair helps to protect the body, especially where it is thicker and longer on the head. It also helps to keep the body warm in cold conditions.

Straight black hair is the result of black melanin from a round follicle

**21** Scalp hairs get longer by about 3 millimeters each week, on average. Eyebrow hairs grow more slowly. No hairs live forever. Each one grows for a time, then it falls out, and its follicle has a "rest" before a new hair sprouts. This is happening all the time, so the body always has some hairs on each part.

**22** Nails, like hairs, grow at their base (the nail root) and are made of keratin. Also like hairs, nails grow faster in summer than in winter, and faster at night than by day. Nails lengthen by about half a millimeter, on average, each week.

Nail root

Cuticle (skin edge)

Nail bed

Bone inside finger

▲ The growing nail root is hidden under skin. The nail slides slowly along the nail bed.

▲ Nails make the fingertips stronger and more rigid for pressing hard on guitar strings. Slightly longer nails pluck the strings.

**23** Nails have many uses, from peeling off sticky labels to plucking guitar strings or scratching an itch. They protect and stiffen the ends of the fingers, where there are nerves that give us our sense of touch.

### I DON'T BELIEVE IT!

A scalp hair grows for up to five years before it falls out and gets replaced. Left uncut during this time, it would be about 3 feet long. But some people have unusual hair that grows faster and for longer. Each hair can reach more than 16 feet in length before dropping out.

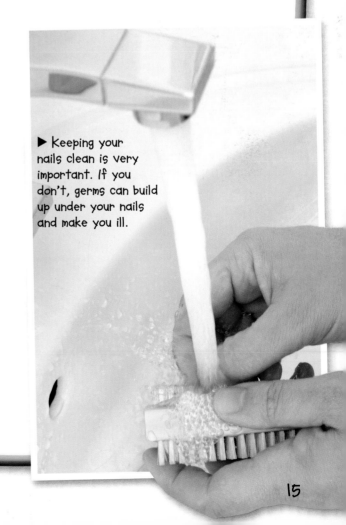

► Keeping your nails clean is very important. If you don't, germs can build up under your nails and make you ill.

# The bony body

**24** Without bones, the body would be as floppy as a jellyfish! Bones do many jobs. The long bones in the arms work like levers to reach out the hands. The finger bones grasp and grip. Bones protect softer body parts. The domelike skull protects the brain. The ribs shield the lungs and heart. Bones also produce blood cells, as explained on the opposite page.

Cranium
(skull)

Mandible
(lower jaw)

Sternum
(breastbone)

Clavicle
(collarbone)

Rib

Humerus

Vertebra
(backbone)

Ulna

Radius

Pelvis
(hip bone)

Femur
(thigh bone)

Patella
(kneecap)

Tibia

Fibula

Heel bone

Toe bone

Suture

◄ The skull has deep bowls for the eyes, and small holes where nerves pass through to join the brain inside.

▶ The skeleton forms a strong framework inside the body. The only artificial (man-made) substances that can match bone for strength and lightness are some of the materials used to make racing cars and jet planes.

**25** All the bones together make up the skeleton. Most people have 206 bones, from head to toe as follows:
- 8 in the upper part of the skull, the cranium or braincase
- 14 in the face
- 6 tiny ear bones, 3 deep in each ear
- 1 in the neck, which is floating and not directly connected to any other bone
- 26 in the spinal column or backbone
- 25 in the chest, being 24 ribs and the breastbone
- 32 in each arm, from shoulder to fingertips (8 in each wrist)
- 31 in each leg, from hip to toetips (7 in each ankle)

**26** Bone contains threads of the tough, slightly bendy substance called collagen. It also has hard minerals such as calcium and phosphate. Together, the collagen and minerals make a bone strong and rigid, yet able to bend slightly under stress. Bones have blood vessels for nourishment and nerves to feel pressure and pain. Also, some bones are not solid. They contain a soft substance called marrow. This makes tiny parts for the blood, called red and white blood cells.

Spongy bone

Marrow

Nerves and blood vessels

Compact (hard) bone

"Skin" of bone (periosteum)

End or head of bone

▲ Bone has a hard layer outside, a spongy layer next, and soft marrow in the middle.

## NAME THE BONE!

Every bone has a scientific or medical name, and many have ordinary names too. Can you match up these ordinary and scientific names for various bones?

1. Mandible 2. Femur 3. Clavicle
4. Pelvis 5. Patella 6. Sternum

a. Thigh bone b. Breastbone
c. Kneecap d. Hip bone
e. Collarbone f. Lower jaw bone

Answers:
1f 2a 3e 4d 5c 6b

# The flexible body

**27** Without joints, very few body parts, apart from your tongue and eyebrows, could move! Joints between bones allow the skeleton to bend. You have more than 200 joints. The largest are in the hips and knees. The smallest are in the fingers, toes, and between the tiny bones inside each ear, which help you hear.

**28** There are several kinds of joints, depending on the shapes of the bone ends, and how much the bones can move. Bend your knee and your lower leg moves forward and backward, but not sideways. This is a hinge-type joint. Bend your hip and your leg can move forward, backward, and also from side to side. This is a ball-and-socket joint.

▶ This X-ray shows a dislocated (out of place) shoulder. The shoulder joint has the biggest range of movement, so this injury is common.

Collarbone

Shoulder blade

Head of upper arm bone

## TEST YOUR JOINTS

Try using these different joints carefully, and see how much movement they allow. Can you guess the type of joint used in each one—hinge or ball-and-socket?

1. Fingertip joint (smallest knuckle)
2. Elbow
3. Hip
4. Shoulder

Answers:
1. hinge 2. hinge
3. ball-and-socket 4. ball-and-socket

**29** Inside a joint where the bones come together, each bone end is covered with a smooth, shiny, slippery, slightly springy substance, known as cartilage. This is smeared with a thick liquid called synovial fluid. The fluid works like the oil in a car, to smooth the movements and reduce rubbing and wear between the cartilage surfaces.

**30** The bones in a joint are linked together by a baglike part, the capsule, and strong, stretchy, straplike ligaments. The ligaments let the bones move but stop them coming apart or moving too far. The shoulder has seven strong ligaments.

**31** In some joints, there are cartilage coverings over the bone ends and also pads of cartilage between the cartilage. These extra pads are called articular discs. There is one in each joint in the backbone, between the spinal bones, which are called vertebrae. There are also two of these extra cartilages, known as menisci, in each knee joint. They help the knee to "lock" straight so that we can stand up without too much effort.

Muscle
Femur
Patella (kneecap)
Ligament
Tendon
Cartilage pad
Fibula
Tibia

▲ The knee has many ligaments, cartilage pads (menisci), and strong tendons that anchor muscles.

KEY
① Swivel joint
② Ellipsoidal joints
③ Saddle joint
④ Ball-and-socket joint
⑤ Hinge joint
⑥ Plane joints

◄ Synovial joints allow the body to move in many ways so we can walk, run, play, and work.

# When muscles pull

**32** Almost half the body's weight is muscles, and there are more than 640 of them! Muscles have one simple but important job, which is to get shorter, or contract. A muscle cannot forcefully get longer.

▼ A tendon is stuck firmly into the bone it pulls, with a joint stronger than superglue!

Tendon

Bone

Pectoralis

Biceps

Deltoid

Abdominal wall muscles

Trapezius

Rectus femoris

Gluteus

Semitendinosus

Gastrocnemius

▲ The muscles shown here are those just beneath the skin, called superficial muscles. Under them is another layer, the deep muscle layer. In some areas there is an additional layer, the medial muscles.

**33** A muscle is joined to a bone by its tendon. This is where the end of the muscle becomes slimmer or tapers, and is strengthened by strong, thick fibers of collagen. The fibers are fixed firmly into the surface of the bone.

**34** Some muscles are wide or broad, and shaped more like flat sheets or triangles. These include the three layers of muscles in the lower front and sides of the body, called the abdominal wall muscles. If you tense or contract them, they pull your tummy in to make you look thinner.

# 35

**Most muscles are long and slim, and joined to bones at each end.** As they contract they pull on the bones and move them. As this happens, the muscle becomes wider, or more bulging in the middle. To move the bone back again, a muscle on the other side of it contracts, while the first muscle relaxes and is pulled longer.

# 36

**Every muscle in the body has a scientific or medical name, which is often quite long and complicated.** Some of these names are familiar to people who do exercise and sports. The "pecs" are the pectoralis major muscles across the chest. The "biceps" are the biceps brachii muscles in the upper arms, which bulge when you bend your elbow.

▶ A breakdancer needs endurance, strength, and control over their muscles to carry out moves such as this.

# 37

**If you take plenty of exercise or play sport, you do not gain new muscles.** But the muscles you have become larger and stronger. This keeps them fit and healthy. Muscles that are not used much may become weak and floppy.

▶ Muscles work in two-way pairs, like the biceps and triceps, which bend and straighten the elbow.

Biceps — Triceps

Biceps gets shorter and bends the elbow

To move the forearm back down, the triceps shortens and the biceps gets longer

# Muscle power

**38** Muscles have many shapes and sizes, but inside they are all similar. They have bundles of long, hairlike threads called muscle fibers, or myofibers. Each muscle fiber is slightly thinner than a hair. A big muscle has many thousands of them, and most are about 1–1.5 inches long. In a big muscle, many fibers of different lengths lie alongside each other and end-to-end.

Muscle fiber

Nerve branches

Muscle fiber

Muscle fibril

▶ Male gymnasts need extreme upper body strength when using the rings. Many different muscles work together to hold the gymnast in the correct position.

**39** Each muscle fiber is made of dozens or hundreds of even thinner parts, called muscle fibrils or myofibrils. There are millions of these in a large muscle. And, as you may guess, each fibril contains hundreds of yet thinner threads! There are two kinds, actin and myosin. As the actins slide past and between the myosins, the threads get shorter—and the muscle contracts.

Body of muscle

◀ The main part of a muscle is the body or belly, with hundreds of muscle fibers inside.

▶ Dozens of arm and hand muscles move a pen precisely, a tiny amount each time.

Actin

Myosin

**40** Muscles are controlled by the brain, which sends messages to them along stringlike nerves. When a muscle contracts for a long time, its fibers "take turns." Some of them shorten powerfully while others relax, then the contracted ones relax while others shorten, and so on.

## WHICH MUSCLES?

Can you match the names of these muscles with different parts of the body?

a. Gluteus maximus  b. Masseter
c. Sartorius  d. Cardiac muscle
e. Pectoralis major

1. Heart  2. Chest  3. Front of thigh
4. Buttock  5. Mouth

Answers:
a4 b5 c3 d1 e2

**41** The body's biggest muscles are the ones you sit on—the gluteus maximus muscles in the buttocks. The longest muscle is the sartorius, across the front of the thigh. Some of its fibers are more than 12 inches in length. The most powerful muscle, for its size, is the masseter in the lower cheek, which closes the jaws when you chew.

# The breathing body

**42** The body cannot survive more than a few minutes without breathing. This action is so important, we do it all the time without thinking. We breathe to take air into the body. Air contains the gas oxygen, which is needed to get energy from food to power all of the body's vital life processes.

▶ Body parts make up the respiratory system in the head, neck, and chest. These carry out the process of breathing air to take oxygen into the body.

Nasal chamber

Nose

Voice box (larynx)

Windpipe

Bronchus

Left lung

Diaphragm

▲ Scuba divers wear special breathing apparatus called "aqua lungs." They control their breathing to make their oxygen supply last as long as possible.

**43** Parts of the body that work together to carry out a main task are called a system. The body parts that carry out breathing are the respiratory system. These parts are the nose, throat, windpipe, the air tubes or bronchi in the chest, and the lungs.

▼ When playing the trumpet, the diaphragm and chest control the air flowing in and out of the lungs.

# 44
The nose is the entrance for fresh air to the lungs—and the exit for stale air from the lungs. The soft, moist lining inside the nose makes air warmer and damper, which is better for the lungs. Tiny bits of floating dust and germs stick to the lining or the hairs in the nose, making the air cleaner.

# 45
The windpipe, or trachea, is a tube leading from the back of the nose and mouth, down to the lungs. It has about 20 C-shaped hoops of cartilage in its wall to keep it open, like a vacuum cleaner hose. Otherwise the pressure of body parts in the neck and chest would squash it shut.

# 46
At the top of the windpipe, making a bulge at the front of the neck, is the voice box or larynx. It has two stiff flaps, vocal cords, which stick out from its sides. Normally these flaps are apart for easy breathing. But muscles in the voice box can pull the flaps almost together. As air passes through the narrow slit between them it makes the flaps shake or vibrate—and this is the sound of your voice.

## HUMMMMMM!
### You will need:
stopwatch

Do you think making sounds with your voice box uses more air than breathing? Find out by following this experiment.

1. Take a deep breath in, then breathe out at your normal rate, for as long as you can. Time the out-breath.

2. Take a similar deep breath in, then hum as you breathe out, again for as long as you can. Time the hum.

3. Try the same while whispering your favorite song, then again when singing.

▲ The vocal cords are held apart for breathing (top) and pulled together for speech (bottom).

# Breathing parts

**47** The main parts of the respiratory (breathing) system are the two lungs in the chest. Each one is shaped like a tall cone, with the pointed end at shoulder level.

**48** Air comes in and out of the lungs along the windpipe, which branches at its base to form two main air tubes—the bronchi. One goes to each lung. Inside the lung, each bronchus divides again and again, becoming narrower each time. Finally the air tubes, thinner than hairs, end at groups of tiny "bubbles" called alveoli.

Left bronchus

Muscles in wall of bronchus

Air space inside bronchus

Right lung

View along inside of bronchus

## I DON'T BELIEVE IT!

On average, the air breathed in and out through the night by a sleeping person, would fill an average-sized bedroom. This is why some people like to sleep with the door or window open!

**49** There are more than 200 million tiny air bubbles, or alveoli, in each lung. Inside, oxygen from breathed-in air passes through the very thin linings of the alveoli to equally tiny blood vessels on the other side. The blood carries the oxygen away, around the body. At the same time a waste substance, carbon dioxide, seeps through the blood vessel, into the alveoli. As you breathe out, the lungs blow out the carbon dioxide.

**50** Breathing needs muscle power! The main breathing muscle is the dome-shaped diaphragm at the base of the chest. To breathe in, it becomes flatter, making the lungs bigger, so they suck in air down the windpipe. At the same time, rib muscles lift the ribs, also making the lungs bigger. To breathe out, the diaphragm and rib muscles relax. The stretched lungs spring back to their smaller size and blow out stale air.

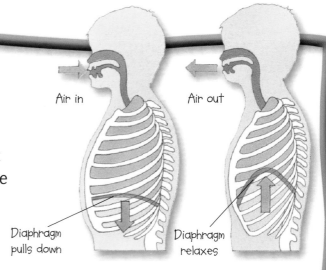

Air in     Air out

Diaphragm pulls down     Diaphragm relaxes

▲ Breathing uses two main sets of muscles, the diaphragm and those between the ribs.

▶ After great activity, the body breathes faster and deeper, to replace the oxygen used by the muscles for energy.

Bronchiole

Blood vessel

Air space in alveoli

Alveoli

▲ Inside each lung, the main bronchus divides again and again, into thousands of narrower airways called bronchioles.

**51** As you rest or sleep, each breath sends about half a quart of air in and out, 15 to 20 times each minute. After great activity, such as running a race, you need more oxygen. So you take deeper breaths faster—50 times or more each minute.

# The hungry body

**52** The body is like a living machine, which uses food as fuel. Food gives us energy for our body processes—for breathing, moving, talking, and every other action we make. Food also provides raw materials that the body uses to grow, maintain itself, and repair daily wear-and-tear.

**53** We would not put the wrong fuel into a car engine, so we should not put unsuitable foods into the body. A healthy diet needs a wide variety of foods, which have lots of vital nutrients. Too much of one single food may be unhealthy, especially if that food is very fatty or greasy. Too much of all foods is also unhealthy, making the body overweight and increasing the risk of illnesses.

▶ It is important for children to learn how to cook healthily. Grilling or barbecuing food is much healthier than frying it.

▲ Fresh fruits (such as bananas) and vegetables (such as carrots) have lots of vitamins, minerals, and fiber. They are good for the body in lots of ways.

▼ Foods such as bread, pasta, and rice contain lots of starch, which is a useful energy source.

**54** There are six main kinds of nutrients in foods, and the body needs balanced amounts of all of them.

- Proteins are needed for growth and repair, and for strong muscles and other parts.
- Carbohydrates, such as sugars and starches, give plenty of energy.
- Some fats are important for general health and energy.
- Vitamins help the body to fight germs and disease.
- Minerals are needed for strong bones and teeth and also healthy blood.
- Fiber is important for good digestion and to prevent certain bowel disorders.

◀ Fish, low-fat meats such as chicken, and dairy produce such as cheese all contain plenty of valuable proteins.

## FOOD FOR THOUGHT

Which of these meals do you think is healthier?

Meal A
Burger, sausage and lots of chips, followed by ice cream with cream and chocolate.

Meal B
Chicken, tomato, and a few chips, followed by fresh fruit salad with apple, banana, pear, and melon.

Answer:
Meal B

▲ Fats and oily foods are needed in moderate amounts. Plant oils are healthier than fats and oils from animal sources.

# Bite, chew, gulp

**55** The hardest parts of your whole body are the ones that make holes in your food—teeth. They have a covering of whitish or yellowish enamel, which is stronger than most kinds of rocks! Teeth need to last a lifetime of biting, nibbling, gnashing, munching, and chewing. They are your own food processors.

**56** There are four main shapes of teeth. The front ones are incisors, and each has a straight, sharp edge, like a spade or chisel, to cut through food. Next are canines, which are taller and more pointed, used mainly for tearing and pulling. Behind them are premolars and molars, which are lower and flatter with small bumps, for crushing and grinding.

▶ At the center of a tooth is living pulp, with many blood vessels and nerve endings that pass into the jaw bone.

**57** A tooth may look almost dead, but it is very much alive. Under the enamel is slightly softer dentine. In the middle of the tooth is the dental pulp. This has blood vessels to nourish the whole tooth, and nerves that feel pressure, heat, cold, and pain. The lower part of the tooth, strongly fixed in the jaw bone, is the root. The enamel-covered part above the gum is the crown.

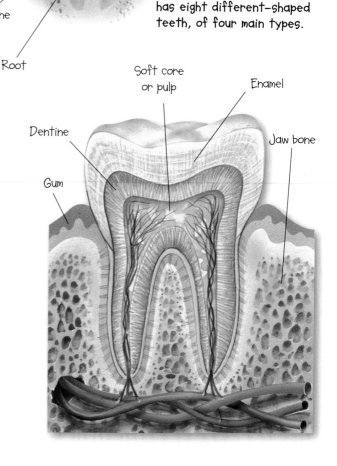

Incisor

Canine

Premolar

Molar

Jaw bone

Root

▲ In an adult, each side (left and right) of each jaw (upper and lower) usually has eight different-shaped teeth, of four main types.

Soft core or pulp

Enamel

Dentine

Jaw bone

Gum

**58** Teeth are very strong and tough, but they do need to be cleaned properly and regularly. Germs called bacteria live on old bits of food in the mouth. They make waste products which are acid and eat into the enamel and dentine, causing holes called cavities. Which do you prefer—cleaning your teeth after main meals and before bedtime, or the agony of toothache?

▶ Clean your teeth by brushing in different directions and then flossing between them. They will look better and stay healthier for longer.

▼ The first set of teeth lasts about ten years, while the second set can last ten times longer.

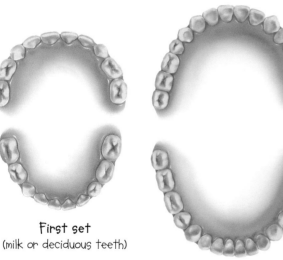

First set
(milk or deciduous teeth)

Second set
(adult or permanent set)

**59** Teeth are designed to last a lifetime. Well, not quite, because the body has two sets. There are 20 small teeth in the first or baby set. The first ones usually appear above the gum by about six months of age, the last ones at three years old. As you and your mouth grow, the baby teeth fall out from about seven years old. They are replaced by 32 larger teeth in the adult set.

**60** After chewing, food is swallowed into the gullet (esophagus). This pushes the food powerfully down through the chest, past the heart and lungs, into the stomach.

① Tongue pushes food to the back of the throat

② Throat muscles squeeze the food downward

③ The esophagus pushes food to the stomach

# Food's long journey

**61** The digestive system is like a tunnel about 30 feet long, through the body. It includes parts of the body that bite food, chew it, swallow it, churn it up and break it down with natural juices and acids, take in its goodness, and then get rid of the leftovers.

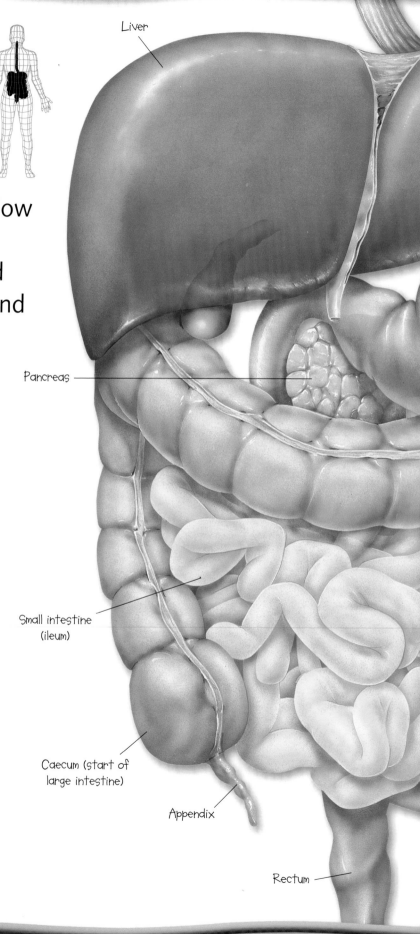

Liver

Pancreas

Small intestine (ileum)

Caecum (start of large intestine)

Appendix

Rectum

**62** The stomach is a bag with strong, muscular walls. It stretches as it fills with food and drink, and its lining makes powerful digestive acids and juices called enzymes to attack the food. The muscles in its walls squirm and squeeze to mix the food and juices.

**63** The stomach digests food for a few hours into a thick mush, which oozes into the small intestine. This is only 1.5 inches wide, but more than 16 feet long. It takes nutrients and useful substances through its lining, into the body.

**64** The large intestine follows the small one, and it is certainly wider, at about 2 inches, but much shorter, only 5 feet. It takes in fluids and a few more nutrients from the food, and then squashes what's left into brown lumps, ready to leave the body.

Stomach

Large intestine

Villus

Vessels inside villus

Vessels in intestine lining

▶ The lining of the small intestine has thousands of tiny fingerlike parts called the villi, which take nutrients from food, into the blood and lymph system.

◀ The digestive parts almost fill the lower part of the main body, called the abdomen.

**65** The liver and pancreas are also parts of the digestive system. The liver sorts out and changes the many nutrients from digestion, and stores some of them. The pancreas makes powerful digestive juices that pass to the small intestine to work on the food there.

## I DON'T BELIEVE IT!

What's in the leftovers? The brown lumps called bowel motions or feces are only about one-half undigested or leftover food. Some of the rest is rubbed-off parts of the stomach and intestine lining. The rest is millions of "friendly" but dead microbes (bacteria) from the intestine. They help to digest our food for us, and in return we give them a warm, food-filled place to live.

# Blood in the body

**66** The heart beats to pump the blood all around the body and pass its vital oxygen and nutrients to every part. The same blood goes around and around, or circulates, in its network of blood vessels. So the heart, blood vessels, and blood are known as the circulatory system.

Carotid artery

◀ Blood vessels divide, or branch, to reach every body part.

Capillary

Vein

Artery

Blood vessels in lung

▶ There are three main kinds of blood vessels.

Heart

Iliac artery

**67** Blood travels from the heart through strong, thick-walled vessels called arteries. These divide again and again, becoming smaller until they form tiny vessels narrower than hairs, called capillaries. Oxygen and nutrients seep from the blood through the thin capillary walls to the body parts around. At the same time, carbon dioxide and waste substances seep from body parts into the blood, to be carried away. Capillaries join again and again to form wide vessels called veins, which take blood back to the heart.

**68** In addition to delivering oxygen and nutrients, and carrying away carbon dioxide and wastes, blood has many other vital tasks. It carries body control substances called hormones. It spreads heat evenly around the body from busy, warmer parts such as the heart, liver, and muscles. It forms a sticky clot to seal a cut. It carries many substances that attack germs and other tiny invaders.

**69** **Blood has four main parts.** The largest is billions of tiny, saucer-shaped red cells, which make up almost half of the total volume of blood and carry oxygen. Second is the white cells, which clean the blood, prevent disease, and fight germs. The third part is billions of tiny platelets, which help blood to clot. Fourth is watery plasma, in which the other parts float.

## QUIZ

Can you match these blood parts and vessels with their descriptions?
a. Artery  b. Vein  c. White blood cell
d. Red blood cell  e. Platelet  f. Capillary

1. Large vessel that takes blood back to the heart
2. Tiny vessel allowing oxygen and nutrients to leave blood
3. Large vessel carrying blood away from the heart
4. Oxygen-carrying part of the blood
5. Disease-fighting part of the blood
6. Part that helps blood to clot

Answers:
a3 b1 c5 d4 e6 f2

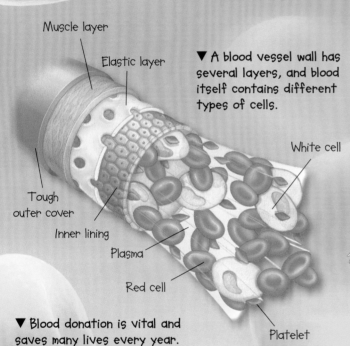

Muscle layer
Elastic layer
Tough outer cover
Inner lining
Plasma
Red cell
White cell
Platelet

▼ A blood vessel wall has several layers, and blood itself contains different types of cells.

▼ Blood donation is vital and saves many lives every year.

AS-1 RED BLOOD CELLS
A Positive

► Each kidney has about one million tiny filters, called nephrons, in its outer layer, or cortex.

Cortex
Medulla
Blood vessels
Ureter

**70** **Blood is cleaned by two kidneys, situated in the middle of your back.** They filter the blood and make a liquid called urine, which contains unwanted and waste substances, plus excess or "spare" water. The urine trickles from each kidney down a tube, the ureter, into a stretchy bag, the bladder. It's stored here until you can get rid of it—at your convenience.

# The beating body

**71** **The heart is about as big as its owner's clenched fist.** It is a hollow bag of very strong muscle, called cardiac muscle or myocardium. This muscle never tires. It contracts once every second or more often, all through life. The contraction, or heartbeat, squeezes blood inside the heart out into the arteries. As the heart relaxes it fills again with blood from the veins.

From upper body

To upper body

Aorta (main artery)

Pulmonary artery to lung

To lung

From lung

Right atrium

Valve

Right ventricle

From lower body

To lower body

**72** **The heart is not one baglike pump, but two pumps side by side.** The left pump sends blood all around the body, from head to toe, to deliver its oxygen (systemic circulation). The blood comes back to the right pump and is sent to the lungs, to collect more oxygen (pulmonary circulation). The blood returns to the left pump and starts the whole journey again.

▶ The heart is two pumps side by side, and each pump has two chambers, the upper atrium and the lower ventricle.

# 73

Inside the heart are four sets of bendy flaps called valves. These open to let blood flow the right way. If the blood tries to move the wrong way, it pushes the flaps together and the valve closes. Valves make sure the blood flows the correct way, rather than sloshing to and fro, in and out of the heart, with each beat.

▲ Doctors use ECG machines to monitor the electrical activity of the heart.

▶ This X-ray of a chest shows a pacemaker that has been implanted to control an irregular heartbeat.

# 74

The heart is the body's most active part, needing plenty of energy brought by the blood. The blood flows through small vessels, which branch across its surface and down into its thick walls. These are called the coronary vessels.

# 75

The heart beats at different rates, depending on what the body is doing. When the muscles are active they need more energy and oxygen, brought by the blood. So the heart beats faster, 120 times each minute or more. At rest, the heart slows to 60 to 80 beats per minute.

## HOW FAST IS YOUR HEARTBEAT?

**You will need:**

plastic funnel   tracing paper
plastic tube (like hosepipe)   sticky-tape

You can hear your heart and count its beats with a sound-funnel device called a stethoscope.

1. Stretch the tracing paper over the funnel's wide end and tape in place. Push a short length of tube over the funnel's narrow end.

2. Place the funnel's wide end over your heart, on your chest, just to the left, and put the tube end to your ear. Listen to and count your heartbeat.

# Looking and listening

**76** The body finds out about the world around it by its senses—and the main sense is eyesight. The eyes detect the brightness, colors, and patterns of light rays, and change these into patterns of nerve signals that they send to the brain. More than half of the knowledge, information, and memories stored in the brain come into the body through the eyes.

► The eye is moved by six tiny muscles, and inside, it is filled with a clear fluid, vitreous humor.

Optic nerve

Choroid

Retina

Lens

Eye muscle

Tear gland

Iris

Pupil

Lens muscle

Tear duct to nose

**77** Each eye is a ball about 8 inches across. At the front is a clear dome, the cornea, which lets light through a small, dark-looking hole just behind it, the pupil. The light then passes through a pea-shaped lens, which bends the rays so they shine a clear picture onto the inside back of the eye, the retina. This has 125 million tiny cells, rods, and cones, which detect the light and make nerve signals to send along the optic nerve to the brain.

▼ In the retina are wider cone cells, narrower rod cells, and many nerve cells with long fibers connecting them.

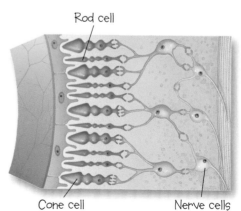

Rod cell

Cone cell

Nerve cells

Semicircular canal
(for balance)

Auditory
nerve

Cochlea

Air tube
to throat

Ear bones

Ear drum

Ear canal

Outer
ear

▲ Most of the small, delicate parts of the ear are inside the head, well protected by skull bones around them.

▶ The loudness, or volume, of sounds is measured in decibels (dB). Louder than about 90 dB can damage hearing.

Atom bomb 210 dB

Jet takeoff 140 dB

Thunder 100 dB

Talking 40 dB

Rustling leaves 10 dB

◀ Some people need help to hear properly. A hearing aid worn inside the ear can help them to hear better.

## BRIGHT AND DIM

Look at your eyes in a mirror. See how the dark hole that lets in light, the pupil, is quite small. The colored part around the pupil, the iris, is a ring of muscle.

Close your eyes for a minute, then open them and look carefully. Does the pupil quickly get smaller?

While the eyes were closed, the iris made the pupil bigger, to try and let in more light, so you could try to see in the darkness. As you open your eyes, the iris makes the pupil smaller again, to prevent too much light from dazzling you.

**78** The ear flap funnels sound waves along a short tunnel—the ear canal—to the eardrum. As sound waves hit the eardrum it shakes or vibrates, and passes the vibrations to a row of three tiny bones. These are the ear ossicles, the smallest bones in the body. They also vibrate and pass on the vibrations to another part, the cochlea.

**79** Inside the cochlea, the vibrations pass through fluid and shake rows of thousands of tiny hairs that grow from specialized hair cells. As the hairs vibrate, the hair cells make nerve signals, which flash along the auditory nerve to the brain.

# Smelling and tasting

▼ The parts that carry out smelling are in the roof of the large chamber inside the nose.

Olfactory cells

Nasal cavity

Mucus lining

**80** You cannot see smells, which are tiny particles floating in the air—but your nose can smell them. Your nose can detect more than 10,000 different scents, odors, and fragrances. Smell is useful because it warns us if food is bad or rotten, and perhaps dangerous to eat. That's why we sniff a new or strange food item before trying it.

**81** Smell particles drift with breathed-in air into the nose and through the nasal chamber behind it. At the top of the chamber are two patches of lining, each about the area of a thumbnail and with 5 million olfactory cells. The particles land on their sticky hairs, and if they fit into landing sites called receptors there, like a key into a lock, then nerve signals flash along the olfactory nerve to the brain.

▶ Olfactory (smell) cells have micro-hairs facing down into the nasal chamber, which detect smell particles landing on them.

Bone

Olfactory cell

Micro-hair

**82** The body's most flexible muscle is also the one which is coated with 10,000 micro-sensors for taste—the tongue. Each micro-sensor is a taste bud shaped like a tiny onion. Most taste buds are along the tip, sides, and rear upper surface of the tongue. They are scattered around the much larger flaps and lumps on the tongue, which are called papillae.

◄ The tongue is sensitive to flavors, texture, and temperature.

**83** Taste works in a similar way to smell, but it detects flavor particles in foods and drinks. The particles touch tiny hairs sticking up from hair cells in the taste buds. If the particles fit into receptors there, then the hair cell makes nerve signals, which go along the facial and other nerves to the brain.

### SWEET AND SOUR

The tongue detects four basic flavors.

Which of these foods is sweet, salty, bitter, or sour?

1. Coffee  2. Lemon  3. Bacon
4. Ice cream

Answers:
1. bitter 2. sour 3. salty 4. sweet

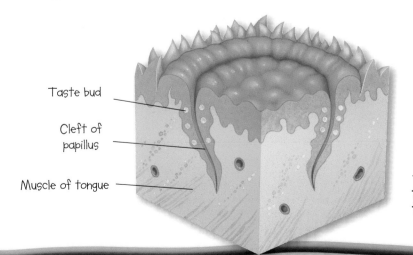

Taste bud

Cleft of papillus

Muscle of tongue

◄ The large pimplelike lumps at the back of the tongue, called papillae, have tiny taste buds in their deep clefts.

# The nervous body

Brain

Spinal cord

Sciatic nerve

Tibial nerve

**84** The body is not quite a "bag of nerves," but it does contain thousands of miles of these pale, shiny threads. Nerves carry tiny electrical pulses known as nerve signals or neural messages. They form a vast information-sending network that reaches every part, almost like the body's own Internet.

**85** Each nerve is a bundle of much thinner parts called nerve fibers. Like wires in a telephone cable, these carry their own tiny electrical nerve signals. A typical nerve signal has a strength of 0.1 volts (one-fifteenth as strong as a flashlight battery). The slowest nerve signals travel about 1.5 feet each second, the fastest at more than 350 feet per second.

◄ Nerves branch from the brain and spinal cord to every body part.

Axon

Dendrites

Synapse (junction between nerve cells)

**86** All nerve signals are similar, but there are two main kinds, depending on where they are going. Sensory nerve signals travel from the sensory parts (eyes, ears, nose, tongue, and skin) to the brain. Motor nerve signals travel from the brain out to the muscles, to make the body move about.

► The brain and nerves are made of billions of specialized cells, nerve cells or neurons. Each has many tiny branches, dendrites, to collect nerve messages, and a longer, thicker branch, the axon or fiber, to pass on the messages.

# 87

**Hormones are part of the body's inner control system.** A hormone is a chemical made by a gland. It travels in the blood and affects other body parts, for example, making them work faster or release more of their product.

# 88

**The main hormonal gland, the pituitary, is also the smallest.** Just under the brain, it has close links with the nervous system. It mainly controls other hormonal glands. One is the thyroid in the neck, which affects the body's growth and how fast its chemical processes work. The pancreas controls how the body uses energy by its hormone, insulin. The adrenal glands are involved in the body's balance of water, minerals, and salts, and how we react to stress and fear.

▲ Sports such as snowboarding cause us to produce more adrenaline due to excitement and fear.

◄ Female and male bodies have much the same hormone-making glands, except for the reproductive parts—ovaries in the female (left) and testes in the male (right).

Nerve cell body

Tip of axon

Covering of axon (myelin sheath)

## TIME TO REACT!

### You will need:

friend   ruler

1. Ask a friend to hold a ruler by the highest measurement so it hangs down. Put your thumb and fingers level with the other end, ready to grab.

2. When your friend lets go grasp it and measure where your thumb is on the ruler. Swap places so your friend has a go.

3. The person who grabs the ruler nearest its lower end has the fastest reactions. To grab the ruler, nerve signals travel from the eye, to the brain, and back to the muscles in the arm and hand.

# The brainy body

**89** Your brain is as big as your two fists side by side. It's the place where you think, learn, work out problems, remember, feel happy and sad, wonder, worry, have ideas, sleep, and dream.

▶ The two wrinkled hemispheres (halves) of the cerebrum, where thinking happens, are the largest brain parts.

**90** The brain looks like wrinkly, gray-pink blob! It weighs roughly 3 pounds. The brain doesn't move, but its amazing nerve activity uses up one-fifth of all the body's energy.

▼ Different areas or centers of the brain's outer layer, the cerebral cortex, deal with messages from and to certain parts of the body.

Cerebral hemisphere

Thalamus

Hippocampus

Cerebellum

Brain stem

Touch area

Movement area

Thought area

Vision area

Hearing area

Speech area

**91** The main part of the brain is its bulging, wrinkled upper part, the cerebrum. Different areas of its surface (cerebral cortex) deal with nerve signals to and from different parts of the body. For example, messages from the eyes pass to the lower rear part of the cerebrum, called the visual center. They are sorted here as the brain cells work out what the eyes are seeing. There are also areas for other body processes, such as touch.

**92** The cerebellum is the rounded, wrinkled part at the back of the brain. It processes messages from the motor center, sorting and coordinating them in great detail, to send to the body's hundreds of muscles. This is how we learn skilled, precise movements such as writing, skateboarding, or playing music (or all three), almost without thinking.

**93** The brain stem is the lower part of the brain, where it joins the body's main nerve, the spinal cord. The brain stem controls basic processes vital for life, like breathing, heartbeat, digesting food, and removing wastes.

▲ Our brains allow us to draw from memory, expressing emotions.

**94** The brain really does have "brain waves." Every second it receives, sorts, and sends millions of nerve signals. Special pads attached to the head can detect these tiny electrical pulses. They are shown on a screen or paper strip as wavy lines called an EEG, electro-encephalogram.

▼ The brain's "waves" or EEG recordings change, depending on whether the person is alert and thinking hard, resting, falling asleep, or deeply asleep.

### I DON'T BELIEVE IT!

The brain never sleeps! EEG waves show that it is almost as busy at night as when we are awake. It still controls heartbeat, breathing, and digestion. It also sifts through the day's events and stores memories.

# The healthy body

**95** No one wants to be ill—and it is very easy to cut down the risk of becoming sick or developing disease. For a start, the body needs the right amounts of different foods, especially fresh foods like vegetables and fruits. And not too much food either, or it becomes unhealthily fat.

**96** Another excellent way to stay well is regular sport or exercise. Activity keeps the muscles powerful, the bones strong, and the joints flexible. If it speeds up your breathing and heartbeat, it keeps your lungs and heart healthy too.

**97** Germs are everywhere—in the air, on our bodies, and on almost everything we touch. If we keep clean by showering or bathing, and especially if we wash our hands after using the bathroom and before eating, then germs have less chance to attack us.

**98** Health is not only in the body, it's in the mind. Too much worry and stress can cause many illnesses, such as headaches and digestive upsets. This is why it's so important to talk about troubles and share them with someone who can help.

▼ Germs on hands can get onto our food and then into our bodies. So it is important to wash hands before mealtimes.

# 99
Doctors and nurses help us to recover from sickness, and they also help prevent illness. Regular check-ups at the dentist, optician, and health center are vital. For most people immunizations (vaccinations) also help to protect against diseases. It is good to report any health problem early, before they become too serious to treat.

▼ In some immunizations, dead versions of a germ are put into the body using a syringe, so the body can develop resistance to them without suffering from the disease they cause.

# 100
Old age is getting older! More people live to be 100 years or more and for many of them, their bodies are still working well. How would you like to spend your 100th birthday?

▼ Exercise keeps the body fit and healthy, and it should be fun too. It is always best to reduce risks of having an accident by wearing a cycle helmet for example.

# Index